Learning again

Katie Green

BookLeaf Publishing
India | USA | UK

Learning to live again © 2023 Katie Green

All rights reserved.

No part of this publication may be reproduced, stored in a retrieval system, or transmitted, in any form or by any means, electronic, mechanical, photocopying, recording or otherwise, without the prior written permission of the presenters.

Katie Green asserts the moral right to be identified as author of this work.

Presentation by *BookLeaf Publishing*

Web: www.bookleafpub.com

E-mail: info@bookleafpub.com

ISBN: 9789358319897

First edition 2023

To my family and close friends who have travelled this journey with me. I appreciate you all and I am forever grateful for your unwavering support.

Buzzing brain

There is a buzzing in my brain,
that I just cannot seem to contain.
My thoughts are racing,
whilst my feet are pacing.
How do I even begin to explain?

I feel incredibly powerful and productive,
but equally blind and destructive.
I feel like there is no limit to what I can achieve,
but is my mind trying to deceive?

At present rest feels like a waste of time,
why sleep when I am in my prime?
My energy is boundless regardless of limited
time spent in bed,
and I am busy trying to navigate all these future
plans rushing around my head.

I feel on top of the world and incredibly happy,
although I am aware that I am highly irritable
and that can make me snappy.
At times I feel overruled by agitation,
but I restrain myself as I know this negative
energy has a time limited duration.

There is a strong magnetic force pulling my focus to the sky,
I feel weightless and free as a bird flying high.
I never want my feet to be back on the ground,
As I see potential everywhere I look waiting to be found.

The colours I see are so bright and expressive.
The beauty is all around.
Why cannot everyone else appreciate just how impressive the world is in which we live,
and just how much love and life it has to give.

People explain that mania is often accompanied with grandiose thoughts,
and that is something which in insight my ambition supports.
As I strongly believed I would be ruler of this land,
which without context, for others I imagine that is hard to understand.

By sharing my thoughts with you all,
I hope this does not set me up for a fall.
As I am not prepared to plunge into the depths of darkness once more,
with the sunshine transitioning into showers as they begin to pour.

Flying solo

I am fading hard and fast.
Feeling on top of the world is becoming a distant past.
Why did this feeling have to come to an end so soon?
I was prepared to take flight and voyage to the moon.

I wanted to see the sights from a different perspective to that on the ground,
when all my senses were amplified and beauty was all around.
Now however, my feet are firmly back on land.
I am trying to reflect on my experiences first hand.

I did not realise that my vision had become so misaligned,
that all my experiences were unique and within my mind.
I had become blind to the day-to-day challenges that we all face,
and my thoughts had been running at an unsustainable pace.

Although on the flip side I am worried now that
my mood will take a nosedive.
I acknowledge that living through these
experiences equips me with the skills needed to
survive and thrive.
Regardless of how I feel tomorrow or next year,
I will not let my illness seize control or force me
to live in fear.

I will draw upon the positives for which it can
provide,
otherwise reminding myself that lows always
come to an end and are part of the ride.
Learning to live life to the full,
taking each day in my stride.

Crashing hard

I felt free.
I had finally broken out of the shackles that for so long had held me back.
Everything was so incredibly beautiful, loud, and bright.
How naïve I was to think it would last.

It is like someone has turned down the volume, and I am fading rapidly into the silence that surrounds me.
All of the brightness which enlightened my existence is slipping out of my grasp,
and I am left watching time pass questioning where my brain will drag me too next.

The contrast seems so stark, cruel, and painful to experience.
But unfortunately, I have enough insight to be aware that with a high often a low is generally always lurking around the corner…
Waiting for the perfect opportunity to seize control.

Dragging me deep into the pits of darkness with no mercy.

Each time leaving me questioning will I ever return?
Will this be the last descent?

Searching for the middle ground

It is mad to think that 3 months ago I thought I could fly,
but then it shifted and I strongly believed the only way to relieve others of my burden was to die.
How did I go from walking on the surface of the moon,
to submerged underwater so soon.
Diving into a deep dark debilitating depression,
feeling numb and void of any self-expression.

I felt my current mood was more of a reflection of feeling drained by the cycle of highs and lows,
and regardless of sleep or self-love my exhaustion for life grows.
If only I could establish and maintain an even keel,
to provide me with respite from this continuous cycling wheel.

It is incredibly frustrating to feel trapped and disconnected from who I was prior to my mind seizing control.

As each day passes, I lose sight of envisioning myself achieving any future goal.
I wish I was not dictated by this internal war in my head,
that corrupts me into believing everyone would be better off if I was dead.

I find it scary how my brain can cause me to question my very existence,
and I wonder why my thoughts reign over me with such persistence.
I wish there was a simple answer and end to this constant torment and pain,
maybe then I would be able to see how in this world I can remain.

The beast

There is a beast in my basement kept under lock and key.
However, sometimes it is me who becomes captive and he, the beast, roams free.

I should introduce you and speak of his name.
But his strength continues to grow despite my secrecy and shame.

He thrives in darkness, isolation and heightens any self-doubt.
Draining all energy and joy from my life like an emotional drought.

The beast is powerful and manipulative in what he wants me to see,
showing my friends and family in a life absent without me.

The beast's negativity clouds all judgement and as time moves on,
he makes me question my purpose and where I truly belong.

However, the beast has a weakness clear for all to see.
Giving me strength in the battle to set my mind free.
He cannot destroy fond memories and past fun, helping me to envision how darkness and light can coexist as one.

I am truly sorry for my absence, but I hope you understand.
Battling the beast alone is like rapidly sinking in the sand.

His name is depression, and he has currently taken a hold of me.
Now you know.
I hope you can assist in taming the beast and securing him back under lock and key.

My tool kit

I was adamant I would fight this beast by myself,
but acknowledge I sometimes lose sight of what is best for mental health.
I strongly dislike taking medication,
relying on any aid.
But my thoughts untamed leave me exhausted and afraid.

As much as I do not like to openly admit,
medication is an important part of my tool kit.
Key to keeping me balanced and well.
Either preventing my mood from dipping as I withdraw into my shell,
or stopping me from going high.
Leading me to believing I have no limits and can fly.

Without medication I struggle to function and go about each day.
Often I feel overwhelmed and just want to hide away,
or I am fixated on every colour and sound,
left struggling to keep my feet on the ground.

Although it is a balance between side effects and wellness,
I am certain I do not want my life dictated by illness.

If taking medication helps me to thrive,
I will remind myself of dark days when I have fought to survive.
As well as the days I have spent on the ceiling,
out of touch with how I was truly feeling.
How medication in these times has helped me to cope,
when I truly believed there was no hope...

No hope of recovery and finding my old self,
buried by ongoing battles with my mental health.
Moving forward I will use all the tools I possess to keep me on track.
Directing my focus,
planning for the future and not looking back.

Unboxed

When you are physically unwell it is common to treat illness with a drug.
However with mental health,
whether by family, friends, or yourself,
it is often swept under a rug.

Except I do not have a rug but a box,
one with no key or locks.
Filled to the brim with all experiences distressing and painful,
the number of problems I try to bury in my box is shameful.

I find it is a safe place for difficult memories to be stored and hide.
However, I know it has a capacity and limit before it bursts open wide.
Leaving me vulnerable and fragile as I am haunted by my past,
reminding me that the impact of unprocessed memories is vast.

Although my box helps me to function each day,
its shadows follow me around impacting the person I am today.

It is like a ticking time bomb waiting to explode,
and there becomes a point where it is time to
unpack and offload.

Learning from past mistakes, I will make sure to
tackle problems when they first present
themselves.
Instead of collecting boxes,
stacking them high up on the shelves.
Preventing them from mounting to an
unmanageable height,
because if I go to battle with my box, I know
who will win the fight.

Storm force

Sat inside gazing out into the wintry landscape.
Darkness surrounds me as the wind howls
calling into the night.
Balls of ice hammering against the fragile
window pane,
My only protection from the outside elements of
nature.

I seek safety and security from within the four
walls I call my home.
Desperate to feel less alone.
For I know what is coming.
I have endured the storm before.
Unprepared, powerless and at mercy in its path.

Tomorrow can be a different story though.
Past experiences have taught me that storms do
not last.
With strength and courage, the storm once again
becomes the past.
Yesterday's struggles are worthwhile,
when I regain touch with all that makes me
smile.

As a new day dawns,

the sun rises and thunderous clouds part.
Shining the light on past darkness,
paving the way for a fresh start.

Sailing away from the darkness

I felt like a ship stuck out at sea.
My anchor dragging across the ocean floor providing limited stability.
The waves and rocky waters were a drain on my physical resources.
As I struggled to battle on against natures forces.

Ships passing by returned a wave.
Not realising that I was not waving but drowning,
desperate to be saved.
There was no land for miles as far as the eye could see.
All I wanted was to feel connected and comfortable as me.

However, time isolated and alone caused me to reflect.
That we can learn from distressing situations what we least expect.
So flip it on its head,
and focus on the positives instead.

For the sea is a network connecting people and places.
It must be travelled to reach a new destination and meet new faces.
The journey may not be plain sailing,
but each mile forwards is further proof that you are not failing.

Hold on and weather the storm.
As the sun rises over the horizon a new opportunity dawns.
A step closer to the old self you once knew,
coming back stronger from pushing on through.

Sunshine and showers

The weight of depression grows exponentially as time goes on,
and anyone carrying the weight of this burden is incredibly strong.
They may not be able to see this when they feel immersed in gloom,
but even flowers need a little rain to grow and bloom.

The challenges you face now will always be overcome,
and your struggles will shape the person you become.
Right now you may find this hard to believe,
but you are incredibly worthy of all the love you receive.

Breaking down the mental barriers and knowing when to share,
can help loved ones demonstrate how much they care.
Helping to conflict all the negative thoughts and self-doubt,
and reminding you that the answer to this misery is not to check out.

However hard, try to reconnect with all that depression stole.
Seeing people, visiting places, participating in activities that make you whole.
Remind yourself why you will continue this fight.
As you desperately hold on, waiting for the return of the blinding light.

The sabbatical

I have been on a sabbatical to nowhere and back.
All I know is that the skies were persistently
gloomy and black.
I do not know for how long I have been away,
but I am trying to piece together the puzzle to
determine my length of stay.

When I left summer was in full swing,
waking up listening to the birds sing.
On return autumn was here,
and I had missed a big proportion of the year.

The colour of autumn leaves a fiery red.
My absence unnoticed,
questions left unsaid.
Although I can see how easy it is for my
struggles to be dismissed,
when I am fighting invisible battles attempting
to do more than just exist.

Only I am aware of the extent of my travelling.
Returning where I left off,
desperate to prevent my life from further
unravelling.

It can be sad reflecting on experiences and opportunities lost,
although unfortunately often it is the reality of mental illness and its true cost.

As my enthusiasm for life returns, I feel less numb.
I am able to gain strength from what I have overcome.
Holding my head high with great pride,
proud that I alone have endured this rollercoaster ride.

Here I am back down on planet earth,
with reinstalled hope for the future and valuing my self-worth.
I vow never to return to that emotional hell,
and I will do whatever it takes to support myself and others to remain mentally well.

Autumn's treasure

Blue sky like a blanket as far as the eye can see,
with birds soaring high in flight up above me.
The sun trying desperately to heat up the crisp air each morning,
as summer transitions into autumn a new season is dawning.

Trees showcasing their leaves in an array of different shades,
the vibrancy of colours changing as the sun sets and light fades.
The crunch under your feet as you wander on the frost glinting in the light,
the spectacle witnessed each year during the firework display signifying bonfire night.

Sat in the comfort of your own home listening to the crackle of a warming fire,
eating all the soups, casseroles, and crumbles to your heart's desire.
The reintroduction of your favourite cosy jumper and the opportunity to lose yourself in a gripping new book.

Sadly, if you focus on the increasing darkness and cooler temperatures the beauty of autumn is easy to overlook.

However, nature's life cycle happens for a reason,
so make the most out of autumn's season.
The change allows space for growth in our surroundings and mentally in our mind.
If you look hard enough and explore there is endless beauty to find.

The lived experience

For anyone reading this in a scarily dark place.
Hold on tight,
recovery is not a race.
Know that you are stronger than you believe,
however much your mind tries to deceive.

Keep focused on getting through each day,
challenging your inner demons to keep them at bay.
When stuck in a negative mindset look back and reflect on everything you have achieved so far.
You may be immersed in darkness,
but your positive qualities shine through like a star.

Recovery and healing will not be an easy straight road,
but part of the process is being able to share your worries and offload.
Recovery will happen with patience and time,
if only you embrace both the highs and lows of the climb.

Taking the bumps in the road in your stride.
Facing challenges head on,

vowing not to bury your head in the sand and hide.

Afterall, darkness can provide a greater appreciation for the returning light.
Remember in 24 hours there is both day and night.
Mood and emotions will never be a constant state.
With difficult experiences helping us to understand, empathise and relate.

Note to our future selves

Sat here in a moment of reflection feeling in a much better place.
I feel it is only appropriate to write a reminder to myself and others about any future challenges we may face.
This time a month ago I couldn't envisage how things could shift,
or see anything that would help my mood lift.

I felt like I had been sucked into an enormous black hole.
With my thoughts dictating my actions,
leaving me feeling out of control.
I had lost sight of people, places and hobbies that made me smile.
I felt like I had been handed a life sentence without a fair trial.

Now however,
I am far enough out of the darkness to see that these feelings do not last, and that the battle of my present is now in the past.
I am proud of all I have and continue to achieve, reminding myself what can be overcome if only you believe.

These experiences certainly have a way of altering your priorities and life perspective, helping you to appreciate the smaller things and become even more reflective.
Shifting your focus to recovery and preventing recurrent depression.
Through accessing support, having open and honest conversations,
allowing self-expression.

Never forget all the strength you have gained from what you have previously fought.
Utilising all the skills that life's challenges have taught.
I cannot promise that the darkness will not cast its shadows upon you once again,
but this time you will be more prepared to battle with your brain.

It can be hard when you are trapped in a negative mindset,
not to act on dark thoughts which you may later regret.
But please do not make a permanent decision for a temporary feeling.
Be patient with yourself,
you are in the process of healing.

See this as a letter to your future self.
To bring to your attention that mental health should be prioritised alongside physical health.
Serving as a reminder that recovery is achievable,
even if how you are feeling right now might make that statement unbelievable.

The tortoise and the hare

When it comes to taking care of myself,
I am often guilty of neglecting my mental health.
From maintaining a balanced diet, exercise,
routine and rest.
As a nurse myself I should know how to
implement these- knowing what is best.
However, the switch from nurse to patient role,
really does take its toll.
As I am used to saving my compassion and
empathy for the individuals in my care,
leaving my resources depleted with no energy to
reflect inwards and share.

I have the tendency in recovery to try and run
before I can walk,
often stumbling back into relapse due to my
inability to openly talk.
Therefore to emerge from a depressed state,
I need to be kind to myself and see tomorrow as
a clean slate.

Rebuilding stronger foundations through being
more self-aware.
Reminding myself that everyone's journey is
different, and it is unhelpful to compare.

Afterall, recovery in mental health is not a race between the tortoise and the hare.

Health check

Mental health does not discriminate.
Rich, poor, young, or old.
We are all susceptible regardless of the life and circumstances we have been sold.
So please be mindful and regularly check in with yourself,
and value your mental health over materialistic ideals and monetary wealth.

There are always early warning signs that you or a loved one may be becoming unwell,
recognising these and acting promptly can prevent someone from going through hell.
Prevention and early intervention is better than ignoring the signs until a crisis is looming,
as dark thoughts can cast their shadows and stop anyone from blooming.

Kindness to yourself and those around you, can be like offering a helping hand when an individual is drowning in a sea of blue.
You can be blissfully unaware what someone is experiencing until you walk a mile in their shoes,

especially if you have your head down and are blind to the clues.
The clues that something just isn't quite right, that could indicate an individual is holding onto life with all their might.

So please do not forget.
Mental health does not discriminate.
Rich, poor, young, or old.
We are all susceptible regardless of the life and circumstances we have been sold.
Everybody needs a little support once in a while, and please do not be afraid to question a broken smile.

Step into the future

Trainers on.
Laces tied, and I am out the door.
Ready to re-defy my physical limits once more.

One foot in front of the other as I begin to pick up the pace.
Blood flowing,
face glowing.
My heart begins to race.

Once I find my rhythm my worries seem to fade away.
As I become at peace with my surroundings,
I can reflect positively on all I have achieved today.

On difficult days I need reminding of how beneficial running is for myself.
How much it clears my mind and improves my mental health.
Getting my endorphins running as well as my feet,
losing myself in the moment and the music beat.

Running helps me escape the troubles in my mind.
Building my confidence as I step into the future, leaving past struggles behind.

The peaks of light

Through the forests of darkness and the peaks of light,
the sunrise over the hills provides a welcome sight.
For when you have been immersed in darkness for so long,
purpose is forgotten leaving you questioning you where you truly belong.

We travel this journey navigating from within,
overcoming the storms and viewing these challenges as battles we can win.
For our mind is a fragile vessel which we need to nurture and protect.
A part of us, invisible to others that we cannot neglect.

Fuelled by fire in your belly and determination in your heart,
utilising the wisdom and strength gained as the clouds begin to part.
Standing tall with a spring back in our step, having rediscovered our spark,
as from this battle we disembark.

We shall rise above judgement passed from individuals who do not understand,
the enormity of mental illness and the challenge in hand.
Let's embrace the journey breaking stigmas chain.
For overcoming mental illness is not a weakness but a triumph over pain.

Sharing the light

I am a nurse by trade.
But when my illness takes over, I sink into the background as I fade.
I live and breathe advocating and raising awareness about mental health,
whether for the individuals in my care or for myself.

My main focus is to stay safe and well,
whilst in the process of preventing others from going through the same hell.
Through fighting my own battles I know the strength and determination that is needed to challenge your thoughts each day,
and how exhausting it is not to listen to their negative voice and what they have to say.

My journey over the past few years has certainly proved a testing time,
and recovery after relapse is always an uphill climb.
However, from these experiences I have gained such strength.
Even when difficult times persist and feel never ending in length.

Just when my brain thinks I cannot carry on,
I have learnt over time to challenge these thoughts and prove them wrong.
For I have overcome these battles many times before,
rising above them and winning this internal war.

I hope through my struggles I can inspire others to proceed with this fight,
and help individuals to see that their future ahead is bright.
With time I will return to nursing to carry the hope for others that I for myself have struggled to find,
and demonstrate the importance of being kind to our mind.

Without looking after our delicate but powerful brains,
it is difficult to aspire, plan out our hopes and dreams.
Identifying our future aims.
So my rule number one for navigating the twists and turns of life's path.
Don't take life too seriously,
never leaving behind the people and experiences that make you laugh.

Life is a jigsaw puzzle

Life is often about perspective and learning from the past.
Sometimes those lessons can be over a long period of reflection or short and fast.
A wise individual once said to view life as a jigsaw.
Often at the beginning you question each piece, their purpose and what they stand for.
You start the puzzle in a position of chaos with many pieces which do not seem to fit together.
But that image is ever evolving, changing- representing that the perceived chaos of your present does not last forever.

As you begin to progress in the puzzle you can reflect on how each piece contributes an important part of who you are today.
Despite how small and insignificant some may seem, you would not be complete if they were taken away.
However the jigsaw of life is never complete.
It may become more organised and the game of survival becomes a more surmountable feat.
Whether big or small, there are always lessons that our life has to teach.

Even if on occasions they feel so far out of reach.

Despite this, as each day passes pieces are added and taken away.
Sometimes it takes time to realise their meaning and that is okay.
Always refer to the jigsaw if unsure.
When perspective becomes distorted it is hard to see the chaos that came before.

Progress is progress no matter how small,
try not to see a setback as a fall.
Piece by piece.
With time,
you will find that inner peace.

Navigating the maze of diagnosis

Within mental health, clinicians always seem in a hurry to diagnose and label.
Often reducing an individual to a collection of symptoms when they are at their most unstable.
Failing to consider the characteristics and personality which make the individual unique, over medicalising any action or behaviour with such critique.

I feel it is common for doctors to often forget, that passing an uninformed judgement can lead to misunderstanding.
Therefore, resulting in care needs being left unmet.
It is important to remember that a patient is not a textbook waiting to be read,
but an individual who hopes with time will be given the opportunity to share their story instead.

Can you imagine picking a random book of the shelf,
reading one chapter and concluding you know the storyline better than the author themselves?

It is impossible.
Leaving me sometimes questioning why this approach is sometimes adopted in mental health?
When the only expert of the illness is the individual experiencing it themselves.

For this reason, in my nursing, I preach about person centred care.
In order to prevent a diagnosis being made which is both inaccurate and likely to cause great despair.
Please see this as a reminder to mental health professionals to listen and demonstrate that you are there to support individuals in their recovery.
Regardless of diagnosis, you will provide psychoeducation and evidence-based treatment alongside the journey of rediscovery.

In short, a patient should not be defined by a diagnosis.
A patient is not bipolar or psychosis.
We all possess different skills, strengths, and a unique perspective of the world in which we live.
Based upon our experiences and personality we all have so much to contribute and give.

Milton Keynes UK
Ingram Content Group UK Ltd.
UKHW020946250424
441751UK00014B/489

9 789358 319897